In the book of Hebrews 12:24 blood of Jesus speaks better than any other blood. The blood of Jesus is the most powerful protection we have.

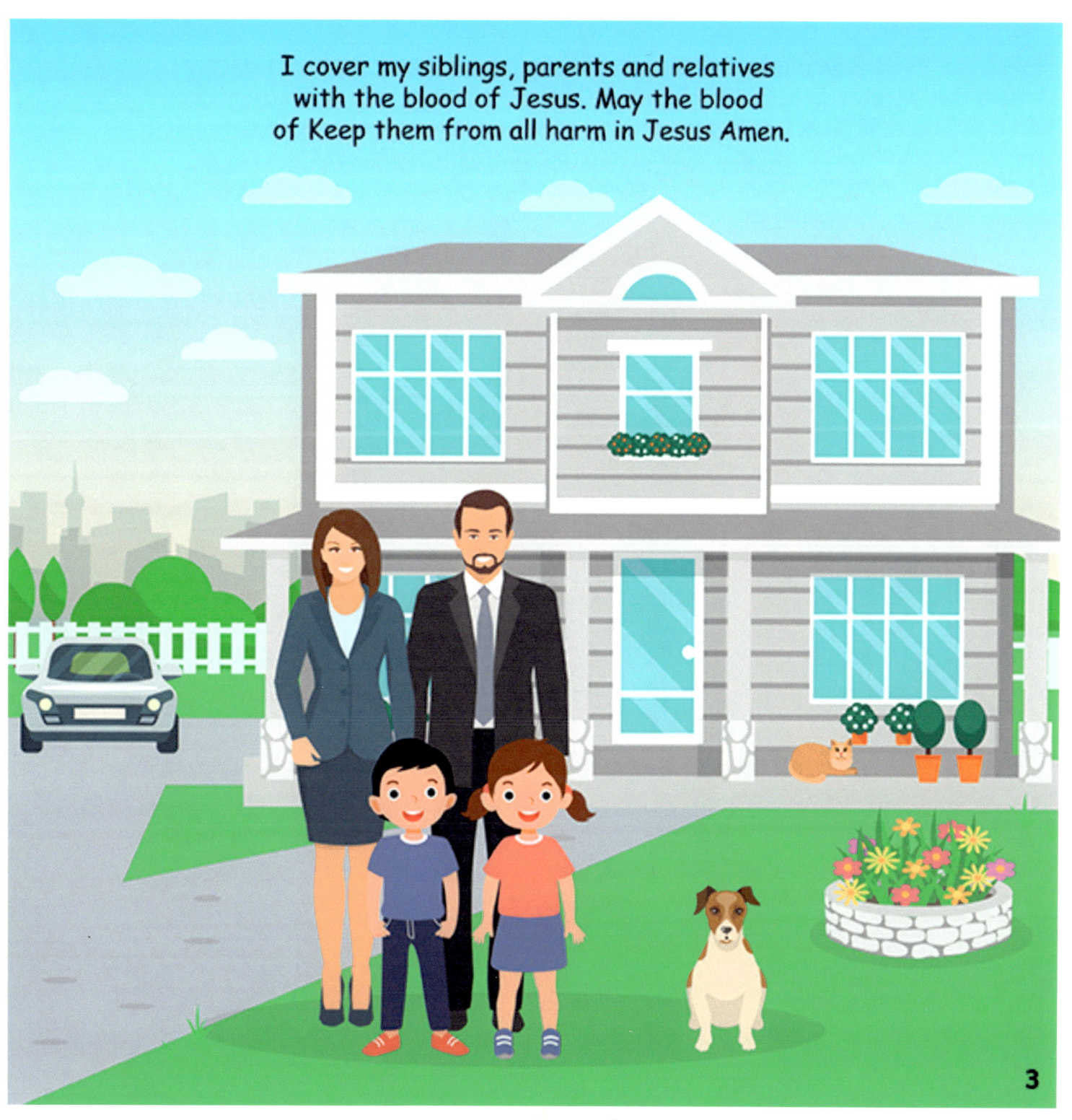

I cover my siblings, parents and relatives with the blood of Jesus. May the blood of Keep them from all harm in Jesus Amen.

I cover my all the rooms in my house including my bedroom with the blood of Jesus. When my family sleep no bad dreams, or any danger will come near us, and no bad stuff will come near our house in Jesus name Amen.

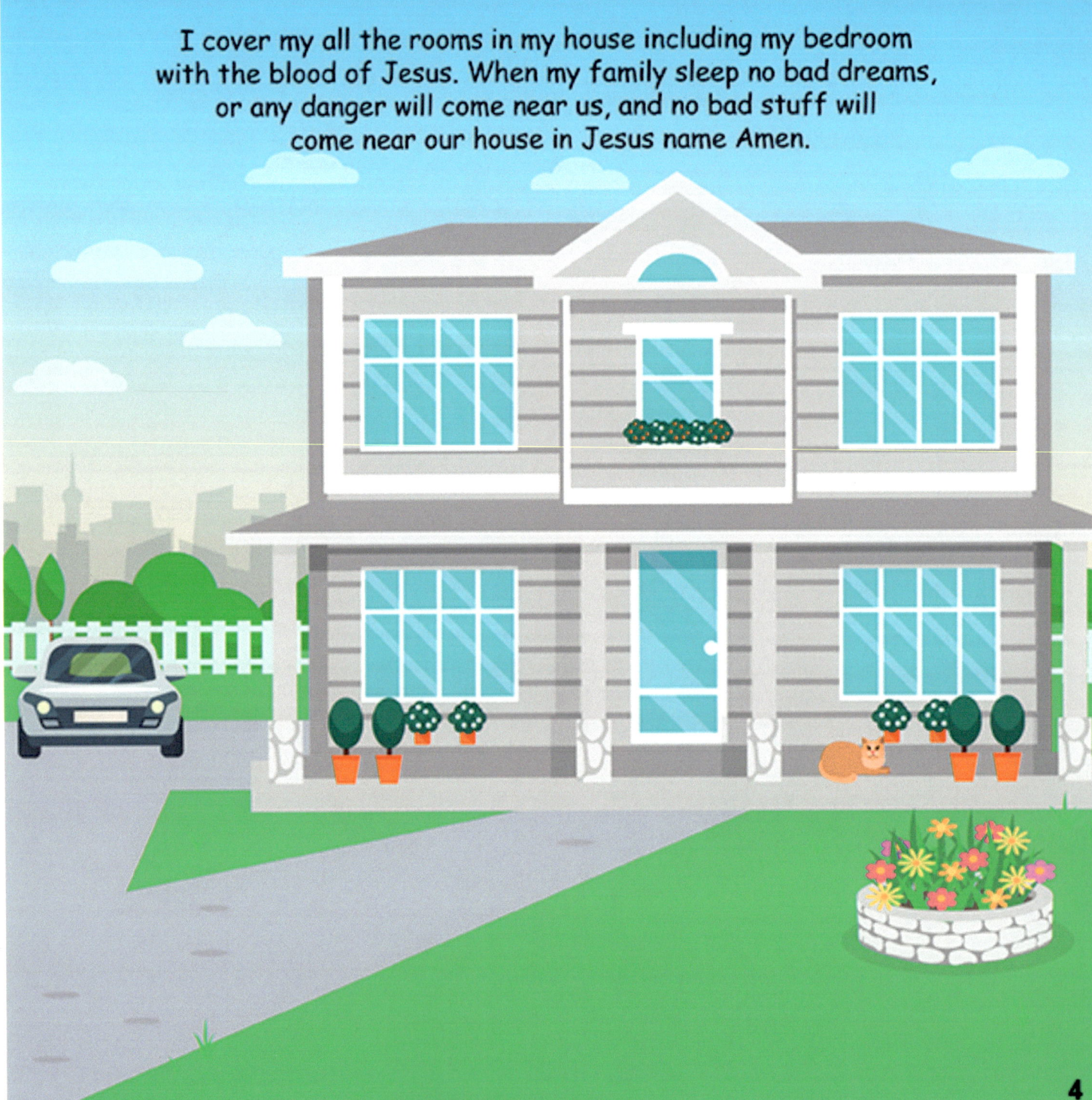

I cover our cars with the blood of Jesus.
When my parents or guardians are driving me to school,
store, church or any place we will not have accidents in Jesus name Amen.

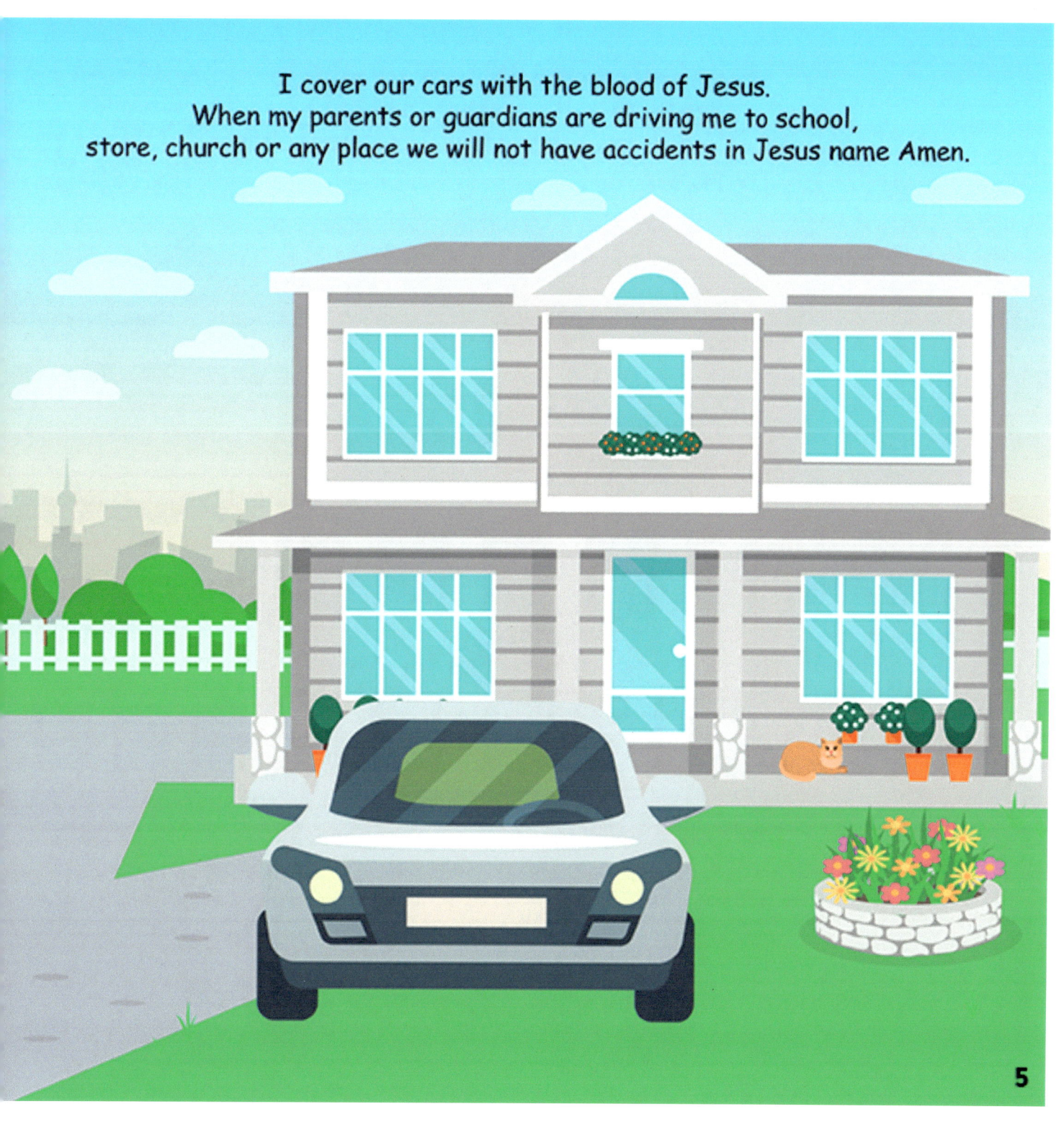

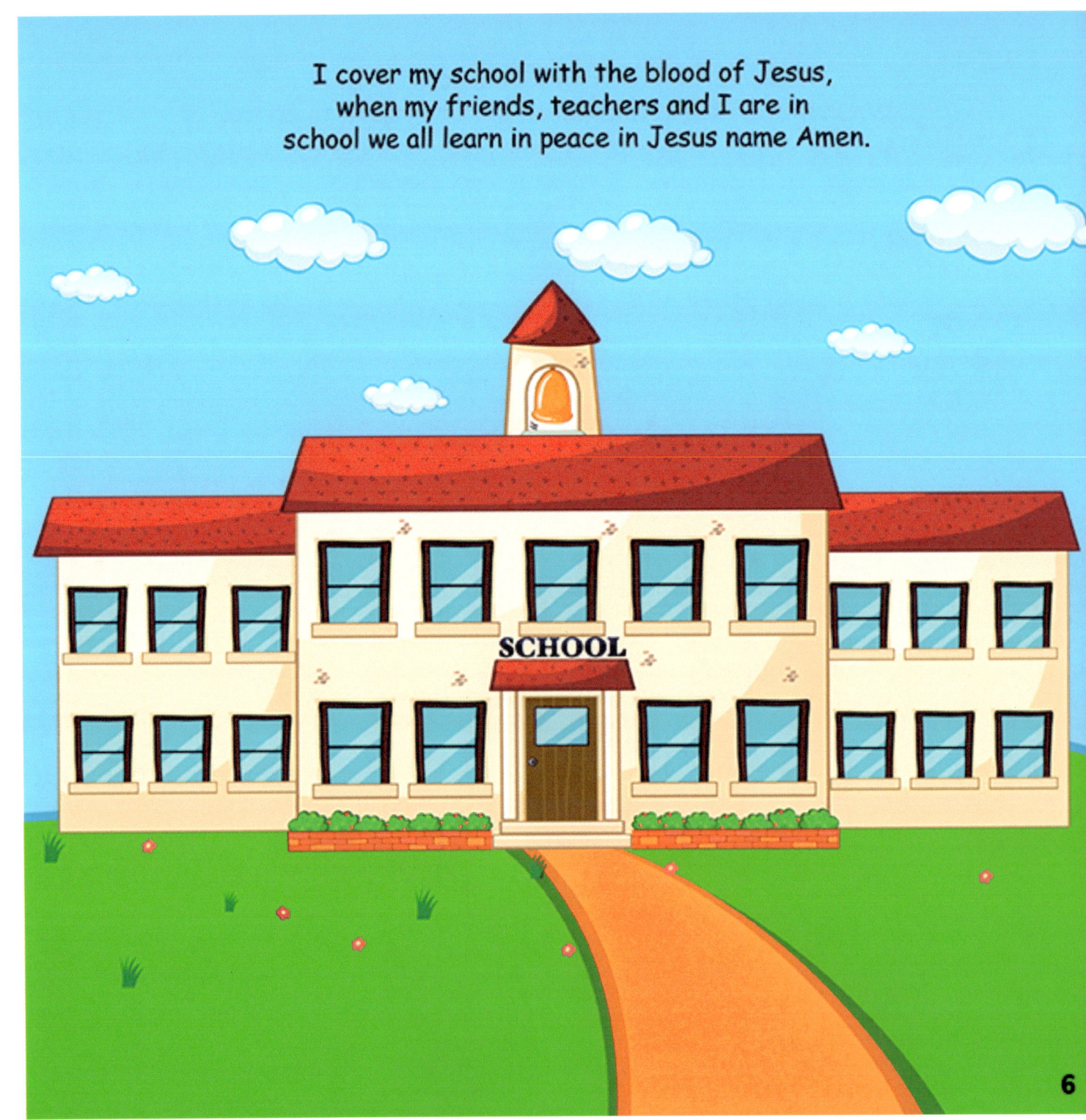
I cover my school with the blood of Jesus, when my friends, teachers and I are in school we all learn in peace in Jesus name Amen.

I cover all my friends with the blood of Jesus and our friendship shall make God happy in Jesus name Amen.

I cover all libraries with the blood of Jesus, and people shall learn well when they go to library.

I cover all churches with the blood of Jesus and people shall know Jesus more when they go to tchurch in Jesus name Amen.

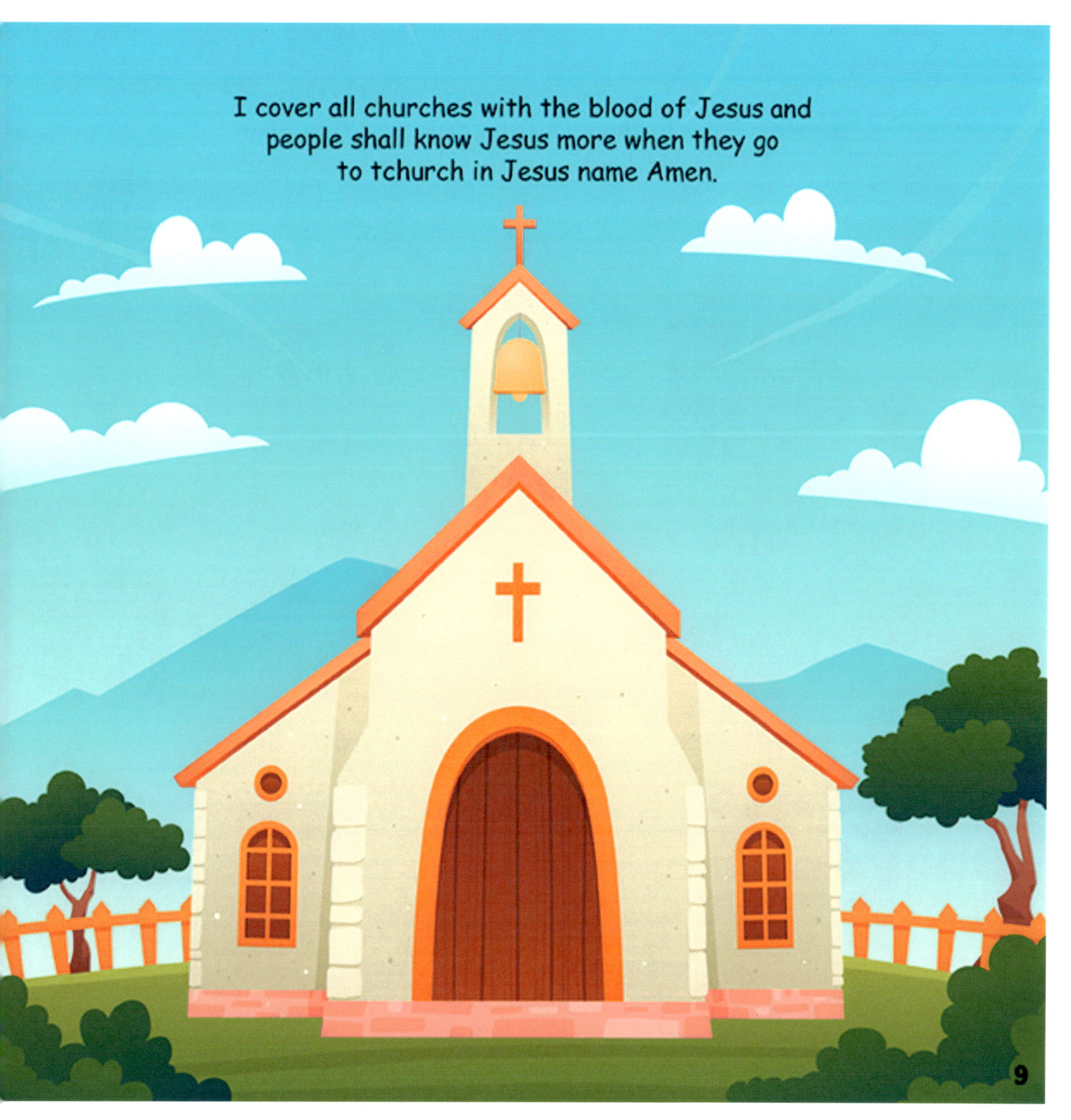

I cover all roads, seas and, airways and people shall travel safely in Jesus name AMEN

I cover the sick with the blood of Jesus, and
by the blood of Jesus they are healed in Jesus name Amen

I cover the homeless with the blood of Jesus thus they may find divine protection from any danger in Jesus name Amen.

I cover the orphans with the blood of Jesus, thus they be protected from all evils in Jesus name.

I cover the elderly with the blood of Jesus, thus they may find peace in Jesus Christ as they continue aging.

I cover the disabled with the blood of Jesus, thus may find peace and healing in Jesus Christ Amen.

I cover the neighborhoods with the blood of Jesus, so peace will prevail in Jesus name Amen.

I cover all gadgets I use now and in the future with the blood of Jesus, thus no evil will prevail through them in Jesus name Amen.

I cover those feeling hopeless with the blood of Jesus, thus they find peace and hope in Jesus Christ Amen.

I cover all natures of the world with the blood of Jesus.

I cover every month, week, hour, minute and second of this year with the blood of Jesus that no plan of enemy will prevail in Jesus name Amen.

I cover all my teachers now and in future with the blood of Jesus, thus they will teach what God desires in Jesus name Amen.

I cover this book with the blood of Jesus, thus anyone who uses it the Holy Spirit will manifest in them more in Jesus name Amen.

Made in the USA
Columbia, SC
13 April 2024